BRIGHT WINTER

by

VIRGINIA MISHNUN-HARDMAN

New York • New York University Press • 1977

Grateful acknowledgement is made to *The Humanist, Midstream, The Favil Press* (London) and *Petahim* (Jerusalem) for permission to reprint several of the poems in this book and to *John Herling's Labor Letter* in which "In Time of Testing" first appeared.

By the same author

THE INHERITORS and other Poems
LOS HEREDEROS
THE INDIAN'S DOG
MEXICO (Text for photographs by Fritz Henle)

Editor
LABOR at the RUBICON by J.B.S. Hardman

Manufactured in the United States of America

Contents

Israel

Night Thoughts

Transformations

Reader, take these words of mine
As a woman takes a man,
Enter this most private place
As the lover the beloved;
In these pages we embrace.

Love

BRIGHT WINTER

New York, white as a bride, was ours
That winter day along the Hudson;
Snow fell like kisses on our eager lips;
We walked and talked
In a white hot blaze.
We laughed as though we'd just discovered snow,
And then in mists of fresh-banked drifts we kissed
With binding bliss.
You told me Gūdson was the Russian word for Hudson,
Recited Pushkin,
Joked about your rebel days and prison stays
In Lublin,
Invented Ginka, a blind young beauty
Ensnared by an old magician
Who won her with a boy's bold passion.
Yasha, my Yasha, what laughter we knew that day
And after, all the bright winter of our life!
Ah Yasha, now no one knows my name is Ginka
Or walks with me by the river reclaiming Pushkin
And a failed revolution.
But sometimes when fresh snow makes the gray city
Look virgin,
A woman watches the ice flow down the river Gūdson
And laughs like a girl with delight, remembering
How she was changed into Ginka by a merry magician
In a blaze of white light!

In the high hills
   Where no bird cries
   And rivers rise,
I want to lie with you
   Free of every limit
   That flesh
   Puts on spirit.

In the high high hills
   Past the abyss
   Of love's
   Last metamorphosis,
   Where the soul spills
   Over the body's wall
   Like water
   Down a waterfall,
I want to lie with you,
In the high high hills.

DRINKING SONG

This wine is old, I drink to you.
This wine is old, sweet-tart and strong,
We saved it all our lives for such a day,
The wine of which there is one cup in all the world,
And from that cup the hour has come to savor
Love's vintage flavor.

The very fragrance makes me young, and bold enough
To bear, with laughter, the nemesis of Gods
Made envious by human love's unconquerable power.

This wine is old, full-bodied, strong,
We did not need to save it.
Drink, my beloved; without restraint
Drink with me to eternity,
For we can never have our fill nor drain
This ever-brimming cup of two who lived
Above the high, high hills,
Beyond the treeline of human certitudes
On love's most cruel, extreme,
Exhilarating altitudes.

LOVE'S DECALOGUE

Thou shalt give thy beloved more than thou hast and in the
    giving be replenished.
True love enlarges virtues, diminishes flaws.
Be family and friend, parent and child to your beloved;
    and if you are a woman be a shelter;
    and if you are a man be a shelter.
Be gentle with thy beloved as though each day were the first
    and last together.

Thou shalt not uncover thy lover's weakness, lest it
    strike love dead.
Be thou each other's servants and far stars, as familiar as the
    morning sun and as undiscoverable.
Be thou an oasis in life's desert to thy beloved, food, wine and
    laughter.
Do not tell him of other men, nor her of other women, lest you be
    told, "Go to them."
Ask nothing of thy lover, for to ask in love is already to be denied.
Be thou in all things faithful to the journey's end, and after.

ONE

The dikes are down;
We flow through each other
Now and forever,
Apart or together;
Unasked, unasking
In love's overflow
Neither is either,
Each is the other's
Long longed-for one.

THE BEGINNING

Without prelude
The music called us,
Without words we moved in reply,
And on a hill above Jerusalem
An ancient dance began.

Repeating the sacred movements,
We wooed each other with the tender awe
Of two who never knew love's mysteries before,
The union of our limbs enfolding and unfolding
Until we were back to where the world began
And we first saw it
Drenched in primal dew
At the beginning.

AT ABU TOR

Jerusalem slept
In its Roman chalice;
High on a hill
Above its golden rim
We turned to each other,
Pressed close
Like two leaves
Of an old book
That will not again open.

TWILIGHT

The last cormorants,
Necks outstretched,
Hurry homeward
Across the darkening sky.
Not a bird sings.
I too am silent;
Once I too had a nest;
Now my wings cannot lift me
Nor rest.

MY LIFE *CHAI-I*

"My life," I said to you
By love revived after the years of death;
Oh I have since died again and survived.
For the time that I lived is multiplied
To infinity by each shell
We ran through our hands
One day on love's warm, sea-washed sands.
"My life," I whisper to you, *"Chai-I,"*
In the Negev solitude of love recalled,
Thirsting for fortitude.

UNMOORED

In the harbor
Boats back from their journeys
Drop anchor;
Time's swift sieve strains out
The day's last light.
Unmoored, my drained eyes
Look for yours
In the black seas.

LAST LOVE

Many have loved me
And many have I embraced
Joyously, inventing melodies
In every key of love's unending rhapsodies
To brighten my dark Odyssey;
But only now does the great theme unfold
To which all else was prelude.
Now, without interlude,
Sound the round bold chords,
Crashing like storm struck trees
In immutable progression
Of last love's total dedication.

MADRIGAL

If I were you and you were I
As we try ardently to be,
Would that still our single sigh
Of longing, each to be the other?
And could love's joy then multiply
In triumphant transposition
Or diminish with fulfillment
Of the age-old lover's wish
To become the other's discrete,
Inviolable self?
The boldest lovers never tell.
So best be it to long with love
For what the knowing stars above
Withhold from lovers
Proud and probing,
Craving for what cannot be,
An alteration of identity.

THE OLD COQUETTE

I

Do I berate the young man
Who wants to embrace me
For coming too late or too soon?

II

As though youth were a fault,
I say "You're much too young,
Why, I could be your mother."
How old he makes me feel!
How chill the night!
How shameful that I am not cold,
But scared and eager
Like a girl with her first lover
Or a greedy old woman
Who fears there may not be another.

ADVICE TO WIDOWS

I

Like great joys,
Great sorrows are unspoken.

II

The richer the wife,
The poorer the widow.

III

As a sign of respect
We draw a sheet over the body;
So too should silence cover
The sweet spent spirit.

IV

When you speak of him later,
Remember to include the flaws;
You are not an embalmer
Whose task it is
To make the dead appear lifeless.

V

As there was a first time
That you entered the house together
Laughing,
Now there is a first time
When you must walk into the house alone,
Remembering.

VI

A rebel still, he defies the obsequies,
Embracing her behind closed eyes.

VII

After the ceremonies and the oratory,
The recollections, chit-chat, anecdotes,
The last condolence callers go.
The widow locks the door.
Someone has washed the dishes;
Now there is nothing to do;
At last she is alone with the beloved,
Clinging to him with the ferocity
Of a miner's bride at the mouth of the pit.

VIII

When the last consolers leave,
She unconsoled boils water for coffee, remembering
The cup that he, proud invalid, brought her
That last morning of their life together.
"Wake up, my love," he'd said, "All glory to you.
You're going on a journey."
And she: "It's the best coffee. But how dare you?"
And he: "Don't argue, you'll miss the plane."

They never looked into each other's eyes again.
But now his mischievous glance surveys the room;
Her ears strain for the comments he'd have made
About the long day's talk and praise. "Save it for my obit,"
He'd have said, "I'm not dead yet."
His robe, encountered in the closet, confirms the fact.
She hugs it to her now, weeping over that last year,
The grace with which he checkmated agony and despair —
King Death himself, until the last game was lost.
Trying to spare her who would not be spared,
He'd sometimes curse his weakness, saying, "You're not my wife,
You have become my nurse."
Clutching the robe she asks, "Was it all for this?"
Wrapped in its embrace, she fingers the heaped
Messages, hears him say, "What a fuss
Just because an old rebel's gone over to the other side.
Death makes us traitors all."

Thinking of the memorial eulogies she wonders, Did I betray him?
He'd have said, "This sort of thing could turn a dead man's head.
"But nobody means what they say
  Or says what they mean anymore."

"How true, all meaning's gone," she tells him,
Continuing their interrupted dialogue.

IX

Forget the rhetoric and offers
To "lean on us"
Of old friends, the famous ones
Who once were greedy guests
At the banquet of his intellect.
Successful men would not be what they are
If they spent time on such as you;
They have important work to do.
Remember, you are nothing now;
The widow of a man known for his wit,
Meticulous of mind and habit,
Should be more circumspect, in fact remote.
You are become a vestige, a rebuke,
Mute reminder that his glory's spent.
Those who sought him out en route
To power have no need of you.
Let them go, together with the pieces of the past.
That gleam of light that was your husband's life
Cannot be held in your clenched widow's claw.

You only tarnish what you would enhance.
Quit your doomed pretense to edit papers,
Peddle manuscripts and memoirs,
Obey his injunction: throw the beloved relics away.
They hold nothing of him, he is gone.
Admit that the work is over,
That yours must begin again.
If ever you were truly wed,
Burn the old sheets,
Prepare a fresh bed.
Be quick, since age is at the door.
Look to the ledger, woman,
Attend to your own accounts;
Your husband paid his debts.
Hoarder, whore-widow, weeper, hear!
The one who is bankrupt is you.

MEMOIR D'AMOUR

After my first true love
I shook the galaxies with voice
Made powerful by loss,
Defying in my youth
The force that drains
Bright day of light;
Of course I loved and lost again.
In time the lesson was bruised into me:
To love is to lose.

      O double larceny of death,
      The thief who in the end
      Robbed me even of love's memory.
      What was that Russian lullaby
      He used to sing me?

By grief made mute, I lived long years
In poverty, on scraps revered
By futile widows who run for cover
From every would-be lover — but when
Your eyes, your arm, your lips embraced me,
Suddenly unhesitant, I answered gladly.

Then was I like a young girl drenched
In ecstasies welling from springs
Untapped in all my wanderings,
As a renascent universe began to sing,
Linking us to every living thing
Until we and the world were one!

O joy in the joining,
From source to sea
In great oceanic surge,
Embracing and embraced we merge,
Become what neither ever was before!

I open under you as any field flower
To the sun's hot splendor,
Welcome the thunder of your pulse in me,
As from our deepest headwaters rise ever higher,
Ever clearer transparencies of bliss,
Revealing the immense cosmoses that lie
Within a moment of love's chrysallis.

AUGUST

On a day when sea and sky
Were one true August blue
In summer plenitude we walked the shore,
Recalling our love's late spring
And its exultant overflow, fingering
The sparkling ring of jeweled years together,
Filling our eyes and lungs as though this were
Our final sight and breath of life and light
And one another.

On such a day, gathering driftwood
For a fire in the cool night ahead,
We paused to watch a scimitar of moon
Cut a pale white crescent in the sky.
Soon the screeching gulls fell silent,
Circled high and disappeared in the enfolding blue.
Sandpipers, small swift wings shimmering
Like silver bells, skimmed the shell rimmed tide line,
Darting to safety as the waves rolled in.
Around the granite bend guarding Land's End
Two boats, white sails full bellied,
Danced joyously across the sea
Like pregnant women.
On the deserted beach
An incoming tide began to level
A sand castle built that day by children;
And in the field beyond, fireweed and goldenrod,
First heralds of an invading season, moved in the breeze.

Hearing with sudden chill the bellbuoy peal peril,
I took your hand
To hold a little longer summer's warmth
And lean against love's sturdy, sun-baked
Tall sea wall.

Time of Testing

TEN-YEAR WINTER
1967-1977

Snow falls on the grave that is our life,
Blankets the butcher shop we call the world.
In the white silence of the crematory
A furled fury premonitory;
In insurrection is the resurrection.

FREEDOM

There will come a day
So tranquil no bird will be heard,
Only the buzz of insects in the stillness
Of a world at peace,
All creatures released
From the old sorcerer Nature's bloody
Binding chain and signature.
If we could clear the cluttered landscape
We'd see the future near.

IN TIME OF TESTING

In time of testing
(Not the seasons of the year
But the stations of eternity)

    Not A-bombs, H-bombs, nor the weather,
    Not will the ice still hold? Is winter gone?
    How soon will spring appear?

But will there ever be another April,
So dry the air *in time of testing*,
When every triumph bears a price tag with blood imprinted,
The exact cost of each atom of prosperity, felicity, peace,
Justice — *in time of testing*
When rivers everywhere cut deep new beds;
When the Ganges, Amazon, the Mississippi,
All the great old rivers of the world reverse directions
And little streams in every land, like women big with life
Whose time has come, thrust of a sudden, in bursting overflow;

And the seas, oh the great, unpredictable seas, freed
Of bondage to the moon, rise up in answer to some unknown,
Unseen planet's pull (or can it be the challenge of a
    man-made star?)

Will they meet again, Atlantic and Pacific, the Indian Ocean,
The Mediterranean and all the waters of the Arctic and Antarctica?
After centuries of yearning will they flood into each other's arms,

Erasing the green islands of man's home and hopes?
Will the end of their Diaspora demand our Exodus?
Is this the annihilation? Are we to be earth's last mutation?

Oh World Maker, Man-Inventor, Daemon Dreamer, speak!
Is this the smashup of genetic codes before new creation?
Or just the breaking up of age-old ice, and will a season come,
Unheralded by spring, more bountiful than any summer
   known before?
Man has no answer, scanning the skies can find no answer.

In time of testing,
If only he could go like some dumb driven beast, round and round
The millstone of the past grinding wheat for the day's bread;
But the grain's all ground, the bread baked for generations
Yet to be or never to be born;
All's reaped, ground, baked, dried or frozen, stored.
Man has his ease, diseased ease by which some without labor
Feast in excess,
While others labor hard, and hunger. *In time of testing,*
There is Eine Kleine Nacht und Tag Music of unfed children
Too weak to weep, whimpering for the crust
That only death will bring. *In time of testing*

The rich are dull with glut, unhearing.
The rot's set in; is it the irreversible rot?
Men and rodents eye each other
In ever-diminishing space; and then — oh then —
In time of testing a terrible silence broken only
By the gnashing of rocks — fortissimo —
The sighs of the starved — pianissimo —
And the pizzicato of fat rats scurrying through
The wonderful garbage that was once a world.

And yet — what if it is a time of testing
And the crashing rivers all run uphill
And rising seas succeed in erasing the land,
    This is the time we live in,
    When volcanoes erupting
    Alter the landscape forever.

Later, when this time is imagined,
Some may say, "How beautiful it must have been before there
    was order."
Now we only know that the shuddering earth
Spurts out black burning land clots,
That steaming seas heave poisoned harvests
On continents fouled by only a few millenia of men,
While from every orifice all mankind bleeds.
Merciless, we weep for mercy as for rain,
And the burning rains come, merciless as we; mankind at
    power's apogee,
In bondage only to his own brutality, whispers the query:

"Is this the brimstone we were warned of?
  Are these the fireworks we sent, like kite-flying children,
  Into eternal orbit a long forgotten day ago?"

Yet, viewed from a distance,
How brightly burns this dear, expiring star,
Loved as only departing voyagers are.

But what do we do in the remaining small eternity of count-down?
Play computers? Let the computers play!
The war game? Sex game? Go-for-lost, final kill-for-keeps game?
It's all the same; but why use men when we can get the answers
From the do-it-themselves dream-proof machines?
After all, the Divine Engine will soon arrive. It was programmed
To appear at the end of the third act, which is where we're at.
But why is each close-up more remote? It's all so much smaller
   than life.

In time of testing
Why doesn't the God of the Machine
Stop the obscene cop-out? Why, why?

Why must these eyes, first of living eyes to see the far side of
   the moon,
These eyes be first also to stare lidless at purgatory from
   within, within?

MEMO FROM OUR FATHERS

For faith
There are no substitutes,
Nor new synthetics replacing courage
As the bold set out into the wilderness
To stake a claim for man against the enemy
In man's own heart.
The destroyers are always
Ready to attack.
But the builders know that their task is
To build;
That only when the wilderness within
Is stilled
Will the wilderness without
Move back.

CALLIGRAPHIES

Roosters

A royal barnyard
Red capped glory
Ruling in small space

12 Seasons

Across the screen
Birds fly, flowers flourish
Pristine through the centuries.

Jefferson Market

Morning white moon
Above a pale green spire
bathed in sunlight

3 A.M.

Silent city
Out of a darkened window
A dry-eyed woman stares.

NIGHT

In night's bosom I lie caressed,
A far star suckles me;
Pressed to the black, bright-nippled breast,
In joyous greed, relentless as a new-born God
I feed content, rocked by the tidal pulse
Of galactic gravities,
Listening to the lullabies of planets
In time's ceaseless seas.
After day's dread diaspora, come with me,
Whoever is unfed, unfree; back in our natal cradle
Feel how gently the night bends to us in embrace!
Oh poor exiled, longing, hungering human race,
Return with me to the black mother from whom we came,
To whom we go, children of darkness, blinded by light.

THE EQUALITY

In death's democracy
Is the equality
Life fakes.

TO A FLY

Oh fly on the wall,
Exactly perpendicular,
Not almost — and not more.

Not quite is too little,
And too much is, for you,
Impossible.

But for us who crawl
On a horizontal floor
Too much is never enough.

Not quite must suffice,
And for us to be precisely
Related is impossible —

And most desired of all —
Oh fortunate fly on the wall!

THE CONSOLATION

To be a creature seeking
Without retreat
To meet another creature's
Need, soothing
With songlike deed
The primal wound and wrong
Of being,
Is to master the empiric
With a lyric,
Proving that life's defeats,
Like all its victories,
Are pyrrhic.

MIRROR

At the boundary where desire breaks
Stretched steel splits, hands falter.
In the shuddering mirror, glazed eyes
Meet the self at last, and splintering glass
Falls like manna-bearing thunder on the hungry land.
Now, when all the clocks that hold wild day in rein stop short,
And time, like a mare in heat, runs through chaos uncontrolled,
Break, mirror, break,
So long upheld by strained arms to strangled face!
Let me no longer see but be image reflected,
Eye of spirit in body's socket,
As sound and echo, crashing, merge,
And the hunted turns to the hunter.

KHMER STATUE

The stance is of a dancer
Who without motion moves
In silences carved between
The notes of flutes.
Heavy with happiness,
Curved lips contain
An inward bliss.
Behind closed eyes,
Green fields open
On gods and goddesses
Gladly at play
In the golden intervals
Of self eclipse.

COATLIQUE

And still we worship fire, climbing
The worn, steep steps of pyramid to pyre
With offerings for Coatlique, womb-tomb,
Aztec goddess of earth and death
Who gave birth to the sun full grown,
Who spins caul into shroud and shroud into caul,
Never saying which came before,
Telling us only the weaving is all.

On her breast rest heavy strands
Of fresh-cut hearts and hands,
On her head a diadem of skulls
Plucked from the plundered dead.
Beneath colossal skirts stone serpents hiss
Guarding the murderess-mother;
Lullabies toll as the faceless bitch
Puts a corpse in the cradle, a child in a coffin,
Saying: "It matters not which,
Each will sleep well in the other's place."

VISITOR FROM BUCHENWALD

A visitor I did not know
Came early, stayed late,
Neither talked nor ate,
Invisibly watched me do chores;
Wash dishes, make beds, scrub floors;
Walked with me outdoors.
The hours passed silently,
Our shadows lengthened evenly,
Slowly lost identity, became one entity
As the guest took my hand,
Made me trace my own unmarred features
On her pain-scarred face.
Then, like heat in storm, the silence broke.
The stranger spoke, answered the question
I did not dare ask.

"Sister," she said, in tones that had no overtones
Of love or hate,
"I wear your mask because I was your surrogate.
By accident each met a different fate,
But pays the cost of what the other lost.
Not till death will your guilt-mortgaged breath
Be free of debt.
The witness who fails to halt an assault
Is never released from the scene of the crime.
It stays in his head until he is dead.
Remember, when you turn on the light at night,
That human skin stretched thin
Gave my tormentors a more *gemutlich* glow.
Remember, when you lie on a neat white sheet,
Awake and sweating,
How gentle *Hausfrauen* once kept themselves,
Their children and their linen clean
With soap of human origin.
Some sins should never be forgiven.

38

"Remember the fiddler playing a Mozart minuet
As nude, anonymous, bruised bodies filed by to death,
Among them two he knew.
Their eyes gripped his
As they moved across the room,
And the fiddler-father-husband
Played a merry tune his Nazi masters called,
Watching his wife and son go to their doom.
I was that wife."

"I was not there," I said.

"You knew," my guest replied;
"Remember Warsaw's ghetto
Where Jews, slated for slaughter, kept their schools,
And made new rules whereby they lived and died,
Leaving a legacy that yet may save you:
Terror shared is terror halved;
The oppressor faced is in that act defaced;
When all hope's gone, defy and dignify.
Their wills were weapons, their deeds
Seeds on which the brave will feed
While there is human memory on this planet.
For, with the Herculean discipline
Of those who know they cannot win,
They gave a new commandment to the world:
Thou shalt prevent the torment of the innocent.

"Remember them, remember me;
Of all the stories of heroes of the crematories,
Remember that small, skinny Jew
Who, in the last few seconds of his life,
Lifted a battered head,
Like a defiant giant said to his tormentors:
'You'll yet choke on my smoke.'

"Remember him, remember me,
Remember all of us, and for our sakes
Forsake your fears.
Seek out the weak;
Let your life be their shield, unyielding.
Remember that Buchenwald is ever with us and within us;
That those who were absent can never escape the pleas
And agonies of those who were present."

She paused; her hand found, gently probed,
Then opened wide my unhealed, festering wound.
Our single shadow split in two.
Before she spoke again, I knew.

"Sister," she said, staring into my eyes
Denuded of a lifetime's lies,
"When will you know me if you do not know me now?
The accidents of time and place displaced us both;
Now each by the other must seek to be replaced
In the eternal purgatory of life's waste.
You are the stranger who escaped my doom.
I am the victim hidden in your room.
When you hear me scream, you do not dream."

Israel

THE CHILDREN

Where do they come from,
These laughing, confident children?
Born fearless, as though there had never been a pogrom
Or a Holocaust or a final solution
Or a sign saying "No dogs or Jews allowed,"
Their small, sturdy feet
Scale the heights of Masada.
Jesting and joyous, they roam
The Judean wilderness and the fruit filled valleys
Of the Galilee's green seas.

Yet sometimes their faces
Mirror the cloud of history's shadow,
The unimaginable, undying void of the past
Reflected in the bright brave eyes
Of the first free generation of Jews
Since the great Temple of the Hebrews was destroyed.

THE RETURN

Not with trumpets,
With tears
The triumph of return.

We have come back,
The heavy heritage rewon:

A stone to push,
A wall to weep on
Where our fathers wept,
A barren landscape,
But our own;
A light to read by
And the book, the *Book*,
The Temple of the Word
Regained!

Sweet victory
That robs no other
But gives back our own
Lost, looted dignity.

After the history of
Insult, terror, genocide,
We are come back in pride
Washed by the tearflow
Of the long oppressed.
For Jews endurance is
Defiance.

We have survived!

Not with trumpets,
With tears
The triumph of return.

A DIFFICULT BIRTH

They said the baby would be born deformed,
Two-headed, weak, sick. There was no father,
The mother was near death.
With none to protect it,
The infant itself would be better off dead.
Some out of kindness and some out of vileness
Tried to choke off its very first breath.

But nor force nor reason, persuasion,
Threats of amputation, mutilation, liquidation,
Could abort the Jewish state.
History had come to term;
Two thousand years of gestation could not be resisted;
The pre-natal orphan, unwanted as a worm, persisted.
Scarred in the womb, Israel unassisted
Thrust through resistant pelvic gates
Trailing, to the world's dismay,
Its bloody afterbirth into the light of day.

Unabashed, made hardy by hardship, the weed of a state
Whose every neighbor was an enemy, grew strong,
Remembering, as it dug ditches for desert orchards,
Those other ditches where lost families lay piled
Like refuse for the ultimate disposal.
Remembering, Israel reiterates with every planted tree,
"Nor I nor my birthscars will be erased;
  I did not risk birth's horror
  To be hate's victim or collaborator."

While diplomats and murderers of almost every nation,
In a babel of tongues, gestures, negotiations,
Corruption, conspire for Israel's destruction,
Young Israel, at work and at war since its first day on earth,
Does not pause to reply. But sometimes, when a grenade
Cremates a young child's body in the night,
Israel quietly asks, "Why must each
Generation have to fight again for the right to live,
And living learn again and again, like that first Jew
Among Christians, to forgive?"

AFTER AUSCHWITZ
Yom Kippur, 1973

For León Felipe

Yesterday they were farmers, scholars, factory workers,
Yesterday the hush of Yom Kippur held Israel tranquil
In the palm of its hand.
Thirty years after Auschwitz, Jews had a homeland,
Jerusalem was calm;
Summer lingered in its amber-colored stones,
The October sun was balm.
By two in the afternoon most Army boys and girls were home;
Only a few stood guard at the frontiers,
Only a few, packs on their backs, jokes on their lips,
Were hurrying homeward late to waiting families.
No transport moved; work in fields and factories had stopped.
No shop was open; nothing could be bought or sold.
Moslem, Christian and Jew, from fear's old hate paroled,
Seemed to share the blessing of Israel's holiest day.

The synagogues were full at two in the afternoon of Yom Kippur,
Sacred Day of Atonement, dedicated to wiping out the stain
And burden of a whole year's sin,
To making the heart gleam new-born
Within the glistening caul of the heart's house.
White-shawled rabbis unrolled parchment scrolls
Holding the rich and undiminished inheritance of Law,
The Torah, bright Pleiad in the Jew's dark firmament,
Repeating its stern, sustaining, cherished words
As Israel, redemption-bent, again sought to expiate
Its own and the world's transgressions.

Friends and neighbors, meeting on silent streets,
Softly murmured the usual greeting, *"Shalom,"*
Let there be peace, the whole land prayed,
In our homes and temples, in our fields and cities.
After sundown festive meals, already cooked,
Would break the daylong fast and song the silence.
Cleansed of impurities, all was in readiness
For an evening of shared family happiness.
Tiled floors gleamed, each household shone
Like a sparkling precious stone.
By early afternoon
Children were restless with anticipation,
Eager for nightfall and the glad celebration,
The simple, hearty fare,
The challah and the cookies made by Mamma.
In a few hours more candles would be lit,
Soon the good Carmel country wine would gleam
In glasses polished crystal clean,
Lifted with reverence and intransigance
"To Life," in the age-old Hebrew toast, *L'Chaim.*

But then at two o'clock on Yom Kippur,
A sudden snarl, a shot, a bite,
Death's jackals were unleashed to feast on Jewish youth.
In Sinai and the Golan, they sank their teeth
Into the nation's throat and feet, drew blood;
Jets rained death on Golan's farms, tanks moved across the Suez,
Rolled unopposed through Sinai.
Why must Israel's youth, untutored in fear,
Learn terror like any Jewish ghetto ancestor,
Be cut down, captured, crippled, killed?

Thirty years after Auschwitz, puppet armies inflated with hate,
Armed and manipulated by Moscow's Puppet Master,
Struck to annihilate the Jewish state.
From Egypt and Syria the jets took off; screaming missiles,
Bombs, exploding shells shredded the silence,
Smashed the radiance of Israel's holiest day into fragments
Of glazed eyeballs, scattered arms, legs, hands, brains,
Torsos, ashes of incinerated bodies
That were no longer Jew or Arab.
From Jewish farms, from every town and kibbutz,
An answering thunder gathered
As Israel's sons and daughters spoke with their lives:
"The land of Israel lives." *Am Israel Chai.*
Too many died in the reply.
"They are all our sons," said the old embattled Mother,
Bold leader of a stubborn race
That villified, enslaved, humiliated, tortured, crucified,
Had never died.

Golda remembered the little Jewish boy whom León saw
   at Auschwitz,
"Stripped like a leaf from his parents
   And alone, without a cicerone,
   Waiting his turn at the burning gates of Hell
   To enter the ovens of Auschwitz."
It was there, at the Nazi crematories
That León broke his great violin, called out for silence.

And that other boy, who escaped Hitler's inferno
To die somewhere in Syria, with his last breath
Begging his sadist captors for the gift of death,
Was it not León who covered the broken body with tender hands?

Can none but León today start the dead world's heart
Beating again in reviving pulse of brotherhood, of justice!
Oh to hear his shattering thunderbolts:
"Justicia! Justicia! Justicia!"
Listen, deaf world, to León's living silence:
"Justice at last for my brothers, the Jews!"
Thirty years after Auschwitz, León has smashed all the violins
Of the world in his anguish.

And now indeed there is silence
As the Great Virtuoso turns away from us to his beloved
Goddess of the Averted Face,
Peace, the Mother forever maiden whom the living long to embrace
And only the dead possess.

*León Felipe (1884-1968), Spanish poet, lived in Mexico from the fall
of the Spanish Republic in 1939 until his death. His great poem,*
Auschwitz, *is dedicated to "all the Jews of the world, my friends,
my brothers." Born a Roman Catholic, he is buried in Mexico
City's Spanish cemetery. A bronze statue of León Felipe was
unveiled in Chapultepec Park in 1974. In his honor the Government
of Israel planted a pine grove on a hillside forty miles from
Jerusalem at Mezzilat Zyyon.*

STONE

Now we are stone,
    After the destruction we remain
    Like the Western Wall, alone.

    Those tears you see are rain;
Stone does not weep nor moan;
Nor can stone be bent.
Stone is a place, a layer of life
Enduring after pain,
    A tomb, a home, an intent, prayer.
Stone comforts small children when they ask,
"Won't Daddy be back for Shabbat?"

    "No," say the young widows, or sometimes,
    "Abba has to keep the terrorists away."

How do you explain death to a child
Whose father is the sun and moon?
The little ones will understand quite soon.
In war the young learn fast; not so the old
Who thought the Holocaust was past with Hitler
And who now ask bitterly:

"Did God die at Auschwitz or at Maalot?
  Or in some far forgotten place and time
  When the first human beast feasted
  On a neighbor's forced labor? Or did God go slowly
  Choked with feces in the centuries-deep
  Dung heap of misery called history?"

Stone does not reply.

A young Talmud student says, "To live is to forgive.
So long as some just men survive
Anonymous among us, God is alive."

A workman spits, "If God exists
Is there no respite from his spite?"

Stone has its own answers:
Stone puts the children to bed in bunkers underground,
Stone tells stories with happy endings,
Stone sings tender lullabies,
Stone sleeps lightly or stays awake, aware of every sound.

After four wars that never ended,
After Maalot and Kiryat Shemona,
The living like the dead are fearless.

We are stone now,
Set in a purpose —
To be unbroken.

THE GREEN TABLE

From war released, Israel the victor sues for peace;
At the Western Wall prayers are said for the dead.

But the perfidious puppet master's show has just begun,
For Jew-haters there's more farce and bloody fun to come
As the Great Power pimps disguise war's hideous red whore
In diplomacy's alluring ambiguities.
The charade shifts from desert sands
To a green table heaped with gold;
War's death hounds point silent, ready for the kill
As their masters bargain.
The price is harsh, but Israel, parched for peace,
Agrees to mutilated, frail frontiers;
In Hell, Stalin and Hitler howl with laughter,
Resounding loud in Peiping and the Kremlin.

Must the Jews alone lose every war they win
To lessen the guilt of Moslem and Christian?

A LETTER TO CAIN'S CHILDREN

Let Israel come into your heart and live,
Israel, the brother you've tried to kill
Since the womb of creation.
O Cain's children, repent;
After so many blood-rent centuries,
In the embrace is the redemption.
Let Israel live and your world will survive, by joy revived.
New foliage from ancient seed will make life sweet,
Fragrant as on that morning when it all began in the light.
O miracle of the millenia,
After four thousand years,
Ravaged, decimated, uprooted — at last rerooted Judah blooms!
Praise the gay and glowing Sabras, with the force of
    new found freedom
Defending for mankind the old shared treasury of
    civilized community.
Praise the root that would not wither,
Praise the heroes who resisted, who persisted in living
When the world said *die*; who today resist the clamor:
"In the name of peace, Israel, *die*."
The land of Israel blossoms in reply.
Chai Israel! Aliya, Aliya, Alleluia!
Jubilation of a people, land and nation
In full flood of transformation,
Chai Israel, in bountiful regeneration!

Night Thoughts

NIGHTMARE

In the devil's head
Is this dream spun
Of which we are the symbol
And the scream.
We are an invented dread;
And all the blood we shed
Is only imagined red;
For the devil's children
Ride guilt-free
On the nightmare train
In their father's brain.
But we pay full fare
In despair, despair!

CHOOSE

God and the devil, in alliance,
Tighten the noose of good and evil
In which we strangle, crying *choose*.
Yet it's the small difference,
Apparent only to saints and fools
That rules.

THE PRETENSION

Unlike death, night, rot,
Evil was not until man came,
In God's own image
Staking false claim.

WOUNDED KNEE

"How can we sell the earth, our mother?"
Thus the Indians to the first Caucasian settlers;
Then for twenty-four dollars in trinket trash
The maternal wilderness of Manhattan changed hands,
Became white property, whore to the highest bidder.
Through war and fraud a continent was stolen;
The histories say "won." It was deal or die, sanctified
By the highest law of the land, treaties sealed in blood;
None called it genocide.

After the decades of decimation,
At Wounded Knee a few Sioux "wards of the nation"
Demand their battered birthright back,
A simulacrum of the old, unforgotten freedom.
Who speaks for whom? What new dooms and new betrayals loom?
How many times must a victim be beaten to be forgiven?
Is it ever too late or too soon
To welcome the Great Spirit home,
To end the dominion of hate?

LAST PRETENSE

In failure's crucible,
I once a rebel am broken, tamed,
Stripped of defense but for one last pretense:
The truth that this maimed, flawed being
Clawed and quarried from despair
Will yet find an heir.

CITY OF FEAR

The demon snarling
Through bared fangs breaks down my door,
With my eyes sees my fear, seizes and subdues me,
Makes me the craven servant of a house invaded.
So too each citizen of the once proud city
Alone on guard against the terror, in turn
By it is grasped, shaken, thrown down
Like some old meatless, gnawed-on bone.
Strangers watch each other guardedly,
Parents search their children's faces covertly
For the new barbarians are everywhere
With swift fists and feet commanding city and street.
We long for the old gone trust
And a new liberator
Yet none but ourselves can free us from
Fear's incubus, the all-destroying enemy within us.

ALLEGIANCE

I pledge allegiance
To the dispossessed,
Knowing they may be
No better in their hour
Than those now in power.

MYOPIC

The Shah of Iran
Is crazy, says Qadaffi of Libya;
Lazily our Western minds ingest the fact.
After all Hitler was a madman; so's Amin.
We don't foresee how
An African potentate can harm us.
Neither can we see
The sun rising over Africa
And setting on us.

STARTING PLACE

After the race is won,
The runner seeks no rest
But, as an exile his homeland,
The view from the starting place,
The zest of beginning contest.

Transformations

WALT, WAIT FOR ME

Wait for me Walt, I'm here.
Before I was conceived
You promised life to me.
Since then we've almost met many times:
When I cross Brooklyn Bridge looking for you;
When I ride the Staten Island ferry
Thinking of you;
When I walk up Broadway from the Battery
Dreaming of you;
When I wake up at night screaming for you,
A daughter lusting for a father
Whose lovers were boys, not women.

(O Calamus, father, fake macho,
You never shared a wild night with my mother,
That pseudo-spinster and passionate rebel
Whose whisper cut crystal.
Terse Emily and long-winded Walt,
How you two would have hated each other!)

I your hermaphrodite child
Was engendered in an embrace
That never took place.
With pen for penis you begat me, Walt,
All the Hemisphere poets to be,
Known and unknown, in your songs our genesis;
And some in gregarious death now your comrades;
I've heard your hilarious chatter at dawn
With Pablo and León.
But I'm alive and alone.

You know how lonely a life is.
No matter, we'll soon be together
On living lips, in the sustaining
Breath of our own incestuous progeny,
The century that parted us erased
Like all our isolate days.
Walt, it's to us the mythmakers,
Weak as water and as strong,
That the world, by song transformed,
Will soon belong.
Wait for me, Walt, it won't be long.

DREAMS IN AGE

I

As death's dawn begins
To breach the dam
Holding back life's night,
How vivid the last dreams
With incoming insight.

II

My mother, younger than I ever knew her,
Naked as I never saw her,
Is bathing in a jungle stream
Near the pyramids of Palenque,
Exposing, affixed to her navel,
Her jewel, her crown, a medallion of me,
A laughing Mayan from pre-history
Embedded in her for eternity.

III

Like water colors
Erased by life's deluge
Are the dreams of youth.
Old people dream in granite,
Enduring as an ancient myth,
Mosaic, prophet.

IV

The family is waiting
Impatiently for me;
All my dead lovers have married
My aunts and my cousins;
Only my parents are still stubbornly
True to each other
Without benefit of wedding ceremony,
As they happily care for
The eternally cherubic children
To whom I denied life;
Now they caper through pink clouds
Singing St. Cecilia's Ode,
Content not to grow up.
Almost fainting with joy I awake,
No longer a childless widow.

MIDDLE AGE

I hear the music
But the dancers have fled
To graves and suburbs;
All but me are dead or wed.

SONG BIRDS

Let me grow stalwart old
Like an elm
In whose green-leaved crest
Song birds nest.

MASKED BALL
after Paganini

At the masquerade all night the men surround her,
None can resist the vibrato of her breasts and hips,
Eyes shine as they sip in her body like wine.
Slim stemmed, the slight swell of her belly curving
From wet welling loins,
She seduces each partner in turn;
And each strives to be captured.
Like enraptured musicians burning to tune a rare violin,
Each longs to draw his bow, with virtuoso ruses,
Across the unplayed Stradivarius, making her sing out for him.
But just before night starts to fade and the masks are removed
For daytime's charade, she is gone,
An old woman walking alone
On the desolate path to home,
Eyes avid with ardor
For soon Paganini himself will play her
In the pre-dawn storm of churning old age;
Only he can make the worn, still wildly willing strings perform.

BEETHOVEN OF THE LAST
GREAT WORKS
Muss es sein?
Es muss sein.

Deaf, old, alone, diseased,
Displeasing all, by all the world displeased,
He hurled himself into the sun's own orbit,
With bare hands from creation's cauldron seized
Raw, searing sound, shaping it into song
On the anvil of his wound,
Augmenting in jubilant progression
The human thirst and thrust for light
Beyond the blinding blight of being,
Himself unconsoled, unfree, unloved, demanding
"Must it be?"
In unanswered agony transposing life's abiding cruelty
To boldly dominant sublimities,
An exaltation new to earth was given birth
By his gnarled, knowing, solitary self
Intimate only with the painful, playful, unpredictable
Violence of the universe, in whose vast counterpoint
His silence drowned.
But then, past the bend to winter's raging end,
As Beethoven forged the last great themes and harmonies,
Dripping fire across dark space
Like new-born galaxies,
He heard clear and sweeter than remembered bird song
The all resolving triad
"It must be,"
Falling like sunlight on his heart's surrendered empire.

LEGACY

My prodigality
Deprived
My legatee;
I strived to live
In debt to all
Who yet will be.
But for your poverty
Don't pity me,
Posterity.
Salute to my inheritors!
Collect in full,
Dear creditors!
You were borrowed food,
Fuel, roof, all the years
I lived and did forgive.

MILLPOND

Dark, deep, still
The millpond
In the mist today
And I beside it,
Unmoved, unfeeling,
Waiting for a wind
To turn the wheel.

ENTROPY

God in lonely torment
Made a world and human kin;
And to the grave
We expiate His sin,
Forever finishing
That which He still begins.

LUFTMENSCH

Ah, the breath is the blessing.
Delight me, frighten me, fracture me, fill me,
Ah, the blessing is the breath!
Enriched, impoverished, jailed or free,
Ah, my body knows the glory of air!
Mine the anarchy of the universe, the simplicity.
The air is in me. I breathe! Ah, I am, Amen!

SHELL GATHERING

In a tidal pool pounded out of granite
Infant mussels, snails, starfish cling
Drifting in bright clusters; a few
Dare the unknown alone, exploring
Their cup of a world
As though it were a planet.
Tiny translucent fish learn to dart boldly
Past a spray of gently swaying seafern
In the hours that I watch their childhood pass.
When the tide turns, a worn, iridescent shell
Is left on the wet sand below, its glow enhanced
Like sea glass by time's master hand.
Entranced, I reach for it,
Thinking it uninhabited;
Abruptly then my fingers flinch as if bitten,
Feeling a muscle in powerful contraction
Assert the thrust to live that I well know,
The unspoken cry roaring to crescendo
Through every pore of my own body,
The raw agony of creature and plea made one
In voiceless extremity imploring "Don't gather me."

LAST WILL

Sea, sky and sand,
Remember me,
Who by no other will remembered be.
Beloved three,
Be kind to me;
I loved you defenselessly;
And comfort me,
Who by no other could comforted be.
Eternal, primeval,
Holy trinity,
Wash, shrive and use me
Tenderly;
I was your creature when I was alive.
Master makers
Of jeweled toys,
Shape me and shine me into a sea prize
Found by a boy's
Quick eyes in glad surprise.
Sea, sky and sand,
Let me one day be
A small child's happy summer memory.